Sideways

by

Heather Haley

Feb 5, 2004

To Bernice;

Fellow scribe, islander.

All best wishes.

Heather Haley

ANVIL PRESS | VANCOUVER | 2003

PRINTED AND BOUND IN CANADA
COVER DESIGN: Rayola Graphic Design
TYPESETTING: HeimatHouse
AUTHOR PHOTO: Forrest Phillips

CANADIAN CATALOGUING IN PUBLICATION DATA

Haley, Heather

Sideways / Heather Haley

Poems.

ISBN: 1-895636-54-X

I. Title.

PS8565.A4328S52 2003   C811'.6   C2003-910171-1
                                            PR9199.4.H36S52 2003

The publisher gratefully acknowledges the financial assistance
of the B.C. Arts Council, the Canada Council for the Arts, and the
Book Publishing Industry Development Program (BPIDP) for their
support of our publishing program.

REPRESENTED IN CANADA BY: The Literary Press Group
DISTRIBUTED BY: The University of Toronto Press

Anvil Press
6 West 17th Avenue
Vancouver, B.C. V5Y 1Z4

For the men in my life,
Lucas and Josef

ACKNOWLEDGEMENTS:

Portions of this book have previously appeared in the following publications:
online at *Bard's Ink*, the Edgewise Café and the University of Manitoba's
electronic magazine, *Treeline*. In hard copy: *subTerrain*, *On The Bus*, *High
Performance*, and *Verb*. Due to the generous support of the Canada Council for
the Arts Spoken and Electronic Word program, "Dying for the Pleasure" also
appears in the form of a videopoem. It is touring film festivals and may be
viewed at ByAnyMediumNecessary.com

Many thanks to *mein leiber*, Josef Maria-Andreas Röehrl, and my son, Lucas
Haley Raycevick, for their love and faith. I am grateful to my mother Corona, the
storyteller; my father, Danny, the nature lover, and to all my family—blood and
extended—Jason Armstrong, Kyle and Bruce Thiessen, Peter, Lisa and Katherine
Wallace, Yvonne and Vanessa Larochelle, Ursula Röehrl, Karen Fullerton, Bjorn
White, Neil Campbell, June Cleghorn, Donna and Diana. Heartfelt thanks to my
soul sisters—Debra Margolis, Cathy Cleghorn—and country cousin, Candye Kane,
for their support and encouragement. Thanks also to my mentors: David Carter,
Doug Knott, Merilene M. Murphy, Kurt Heintz, Victor Noel and Alma Lee.

Special thanks:
To friends and associates: Jon Wrasse, St. Teresa Stone, Pamela Ward,
Sherry McGarvie, Raquel Alvaro, Grant and Rebecca McLure, Madeleine Duff,
Alexandra Oliver, Lincoln Clarkes, Jamie Reid, Kedrick James, Katrin Bowen,
Jim Andrews, Geoff Inverarity, Jhim Pattison, Susan Musgrave, Maryse de la
Giroday, bill bissett, Wendy Merkley, Sheri-D Wilson, Hank Bull, Jill Battson,
Michael Turner and Hilary Peach.

To Penny Duane, Loranne Brown, Terry Shaw, Diana Mohrsen, Lee Beliveau,
Darlene Meilleur, Wayne Ralph and Lois J. Petersen of *Bard's Ink*, for their
enthusiasm and encouragement of my work, poetry and prose.

To Brian Kaufman and Anvil Press, for their staunch advocacy of the emerging
author.

CONTENTS

SIDEWAYS

Where Sins Are More Sinful

A river flows down to the Atlantic—
the Matapedia—
Irish and cathedral
on one side,
Québecois and cathedral
on the other.
They all know sin.

Jeanette walked to the pier
every day to buy a lobster,
hid the quarts of beer
from brothers
Ed and Reggie
in the toilet tank.
Hung a rosary there,
to atone for the bastard
she nourished with
lobster and beer.

Tiny filigree iron cross
laced with lines of rust.

Uranium Town

I never joined the Girl Guides,
NDP or Greenpeace.
There are millions of others
to do that, millions more worthy,
though I inspired a movement
the day I was born—the MSQ—
Mothers for the Status Quo.
We didn't know who my father was
but my mother was head of the MSQ
and I was born pink and healthy
in spite of the letter she received
warning of a kidnap plot.
She always had her suspicions
about the travellers and strangers
that passed through Uranium Town.
They came to complain
about the mine,
sang protest songs
on the steps of the municipal hall,
their demonstrations broadcast
with cutting edge technology.
She memorized their faces,
reviled their phony passion.
Taking our town hostage, she said,
they were the harbingers of doom.
We would simply wait out
the conflicts, skirmishes, coups,
desert storms and CNN theme songs.

We were not frightened
of anything so far away.
I was born pink and healthy,
in spite of everything.

Scrub

On a sandlot of tiny thugs
I stood at bat,
a bare-limbed tree,
fists on cherry wood,
legs ready to bolt.
I kept my eye
on the ball
but it hit me
like a magic bus.
Lost all my bases,
slept on a new bed,
bore a function at last:
a gold cross passed down
for the journey.

In one day
I became the banana boat,
brimming with seed,
steaming down the Amazon.
You're a woman now,
they said, normal.
Game over;
my trunk, the core,
up for grabs,
my body a fissure in a field of corn,
rotten as Eve's
ripe
as a hard green peach.

The Great Northwest

The raven landed sideways
on the hot, radio factory roof,
dropping the shiny object
as if grasping it was only
an empty beer can.

Right side up,
King of the Airwaves
sat in a booth,
raving to his jades
outside the law.
Who belongs here
and, who was here first?
Cruising down the I-5 in their pickups,
intent on spiking the melting pot
with one-irons and crowbars,
his European-descendant fans
curse the tree-hugging Commies.

The Great Northwest,
like a ramshackle farm,
a compound of backbiting,
inbreeding, dog fighting mutations,
strays, nags and illegals
neatly harpooned
upon syringes of lethal dope.
Tugboat Andy is your man then.
Tugboat Andy *is* the man,

the man
happy to haul
booms of loathing.

They linger
beneath a bare light bulb
in a cold, smoke-filled garage,
as if in a trance,
as close to ecstasy
as they can stand.

Lightning strikes the tavern
next day. A conspiracy
of the FBI, the government,
a consortium
of Jewish bankers
and media moguls.
There are no acts of God.

Survivors trundle down
to salvage
what they can,
retire to the ranch,
sink their teeth
into a night's sleep,
dream
of their right-as-white mission.

Maybe it's something in the water.

Sum of the Parts

I sit on the fence, tomboy
pondering the plight
of the eunuch,
the pinto, recently gelded.
The studs nip, nag and ride him
till he nearly breaks his leg
in a badger hole.

His altered state
spooks the stallions.
I am too young
to know the difference
but they know,
as well as any male,
how heady the power is,
how it lathers beneath a mount,
how hard it is to navigate
with worn out flanks at half-mast,
spurs more shiny than solid.

I gnaw on a stalk of flax,
spitting up pieces of us.
Body parts add up
to carcass value,
cheval,
reason enough
to detract, degrade, distort.

Kick gone,
the pinto cowers beneath the oak,
sunshine streaming through his skeleton
onto a plain that no longer exists.

Now

Now.
Now is the time.
Now is the time to say it
but now is the time to say it,
there are no words,
eternally,
now.

You were a godsend.
I would never tell you.
A sports car figured into it.
We drove off together,
gravity collapsing,
howling and cooing
for there are no words.
I didn't know
you were pure, untainted,
a boy in wolf's clothing.
I knew you liked red meat,
would never tell me I'm divine.

I do not want to forgive
but you are free
from guilt
and there are no words
to wipe the slate clean.

You have a theory about us
and non-linear time.
You see us at the end of a tunnel,
doing things we've never done.

We buy a shotgun painting,
erect cooling towers,
cave houses,
and search for Beefheart
in the desert.

When?
Eternally.
Now.
There are no words
but now is the time to say it.
Now is the time to say it.
Now is the time.
Now.

Lena

The red box on her desk
contains a lock of Kurt's hair.
She will not reveal how she got it.
He would take it on the road,
never hid that from her.
She hears Nirvana everywhere.

Another unsullied,
though tormented
artistic genius has hit town,
rekindled her lust.
She spends evenings pacing,
suspecting the worst.
She knows her rival
possesses a serene beauty
that belies a black heart.

Who's giving him head now?
That rank low-life waitress bitch
with the fake yellow pussy,
or the married hairdresser
with the personality of a gnat?
Maybe both?
He's a dog,
two birds with one prick,
something completely different
every night, just his style.

Ever had a blonde moment?
Lena shuts down,
wincing in exquisite pain,
the love he gave,
so much beer swill,
a joke sans the punch line.
Who or what
could he possibly hold dear?

Lena glares at the ants
marching down the wall in formation,
indulging herself
with the luxury of regret.
Faithful no more,
she paints the red box black.

Horse Sense

There was always music in the air
at High Stakes Park.
I heard it in the winning cheers,
the sighs of resignation,
Dad's tickets fluttering to the ground.

I had no money riding,
my picks rarely placed,
but the day *My Girlfriend* showed,
I really raked it in.
She paraded by
in braids, satin ruffles,
jockeys biting at the bit.
If couples were made of three,
we'd make the perfect one.
After the races,
horse and owner
dug me out of the turf
of the Winner's Circle,
took me home
like a trophy.

They removed the blinkers,
drilled me
with a lot of horse sense,
said I'm like a sunflower,
that I *can* take the heat.

Get on the right track missy,
wager only
what you can afford to lose.

I learned how to flaunt it,
stay in the saddle,
beat the odds,
whip the punters and also-rans.

Dying for the Pleasure

I know it's wrong, but I love you,
love getting our kicks together.
I can't keep my hands off you.
I know it's wrong, but I love you,
evil that is mine, evil *de rigueur*.

I love you.
I love to crawl inside you,
so smooth and automatic.
I love to cruise
down the boulevard
on long, languid nights,
salt on the sea air,
eucalyptus leaves,
black leather bucket seats,
me so cool inside.

Moonlight humping
in the back seat;
time to lose it,
time to cut milk teeth
on someone's anatomy
before they became
the jaws of death,
before I became too driven.
It was love:
gallant, silver, visored
Pontiac Chieftain De Luxe.

It was love:
cherry Mercury Comet,
Haley's Comet,
insides burning so much blue,
street urchins couldn't stomach you.
It was love:
white Audi Fox that ran like a deer,
broke down like a neurotic girlfriend
every one hundred miles.

Dark sapphire blue Plymouth Duster,
carload of virgins,
lowlands of Surrey,
hell-bent on losing our season;
all our deeds,
the unseen road
slick with Calona Red.

Sudden, slow-mo fishtailing,
wipers taunting, groaning,
now you're gonna die
now you're gonna die
now you're gonna die
now you're gonna die.

Duster spinning, sailing
to a lone hardwood
gleaming in the headlights;
a chorus of screams
rising in decibel,
rising in awe.

Hell if I'm going to die in a ditch.
I crept through brambles,
right arm a dog's hind leg,
cursed, *Jesus*; tore myself
from clinging blackberry vines,
hands of the Reaper,
claws clutching,
not quite ready to let go,
human blood puddling,
bodies strewn, staggering,
crying out, *Mama*.

I know it's wrong,
but I love you.
I still love you.
You're a Volvo now,
I'm a big mama,
suburban sub-Rosa soccer mom
cranking up Björk, "Army of Me,"
cursing out the road-hogging cretins.

I love you,
high maintenance metal Venus.
You get me where I'm going.
I'm a lovesick woman driver,
in dread of the bus,
afraid of dying in a car.
I love to crawl inside you
though I've nearly died for the pleasure.

I love you,
and you know,
I hate you.
I hate you
for belching and farting.
I hate that slimy, black Puffins
lay white, speckled eggs
on tarred and feathered beaches,
that blood and oil
flood the desert.
I hate this jones
for fossil fuel.
I hate you,
you brutal,
life-blood sucking
hunk
of regurgitated steel.

Europa

Resident alien, distant planet,
two moons, world of fickle shadows,
every surface hard, reflective, argentine.
The name did not confer grace
or luminosity as her mother had hoped.
Europa was born ready,
rough-riding bareback
between the crags, solenoid spires,
casting her pearls before celestial swine.
She's at that age, you know.
Gryphon, sugar skull moon,
though smaller, is menacing and *alive*.
Together the two moons reflect their light
across the face of things,
create a silhouette of Europa nude,
running with the hounds.
She lights upon the waves
like a skipping stone,
dreading what subterranean life forms
might inhabit the lake crater.
The fish have ears,
the water simmers like chowder.
She obsesses over her tiny tits,
budding at a turtle's pace in penumbra.
It's tough growing up in the dark
like a mushroom.
She wants a suntan,
a vegetable patch, Earth.

Somewhere in the universe
sun-kissed walnut trees grow,
bonfires of love burn.
She gets postcards.

When will I be loved?
Desire pierces twilight sleep,
shivers like pampas grass,
her lover a spectre in the dunes,
her life a cool bower,
no one at the gate.

Peaches

Peaches curses her thighs
as the Platters croon,
walks to the Pepper Mill Bar
in the rain,
tries not to think about it
beneath her pink umbrella,
cherished Shanghai blue cocktail dress
dripped upon.
Grade 7 bullies fling stolen grapes,
call her "Fatso."
She tries not to think about it,
scurries down Cherry Lane,
vowing to dance the pounds away by March.
Richard Simmons is sweet
but not as sweet as Andy.
Andy was not her honey this morning though.
Rather, he was cranky, toasted.
He always calls her "Sweetheart,"
but not this morning.
Has Andy lost sight
of her inner beauty?
"You're a nut!" he said,
like it was a bad thing.
He's going south again.
The ruler of her soul kitchen
is hitting the road
in search of ancient spice routes
and the perfect pantry.

She tries not to think about it.
Things are not so simple
by the light of day.
Peaches craves warm hearth bread,
fragrant with rosemary,
drizzled with olive oil.
She tries not to think about it,
prepares to strip off a pole,
but can't help thinking,
I thought I knew
the way to a man's heart.

Working Girl's Prayer

Hey, girlfriend!
DOA plays the Mabuhay tonight,
just left Joey Shithead standing on Castro.
Not much in the way of queer bait.
Slow night.
I'll die a virgin at this rate.

I'll blow you.
Just kidding.
Everybody pays.
Maybe it's the hair on your palms
or that Cain and Abel tattoo.
Christ, some Jesus freak
tried to save me today.
Shoved a card in my face.
Laminated. See.
Virgin Mary on the front,
Working Girl's Prayer on the back.
Hah! That's me all right.
Working girl.

One too many bedfellows,
three in the bush
and so many goddamned choices,
goddamit it.
Hey, let's go to midnight mass.
You're the only Catholic I know.

I'm lapsed honey and, why bother?
You're on your knees half the time anyway.

You know *why* the Virgin Mary is everywhere?
Goddess worship. Not for protection.
She doesn't protect me.

What do you have to atone for anyway?
You're an angel in my book.

I had an abortion. Today.
Yeah, really.
Left my foetus in San Francisco.

I shove in a tampon,
lurch to confession.
Father Pritchard reminds me,
"God made the first blood sacrifice.
What you did was infanticide. A sin.
Go home and talk to your little baby.
Ask his forgiveness."

Moll

I want you.
The strokes
of a weary old moll
lie wilting on the sheet.
On her knees,
sober or drunk,
bad as a hooker
too lame to technique,
she docs not participate
in their love,
she aborts it,
over and over
until life resembles a barren plain.
She sees the blood on her hands,
hears a rushing sound in her head.
Or is that a flushing sound?

She orchestrates her suffering,
every betrayal,
demon,
disorder.
The most flagrant part of the hoax
is her smile, eternally inviting,
especially to men,
then the voice:
warm, languid as molasses.

At the party of an associate,
she stops at his child's crib.
Why doesn't it learn to walk?
I learned to walk
with my hands
tied behind my back.
I lied so that my son
could keep his distance.
The one that got away . . .
known only through fleeting rumours,
the blustering of red-faced men.

He never has to witness me,
the fuck-up, fucking up
or inherit the velvet paintings.
I let him down,
gently.

In the Flesh

He is like the rest of humanity,
horning his way in;
sweet, relentless,
randy as a bull.
He says, "I love you,"
as if it were a solution,
a beginning, a promise.
I am engaged, forever,
but he comes when I call him.

I want to leave,
kiss his ass goodbye
but cannot find my clothes.
He pretends to walk on water,
claims to be the son of God—
his *other* son.
He blames everything
on bad acting
or California Bauhaus.
He goes *Ho Ho Ho*,
as I slither out the door,
has me under surveillance
for Christmas
but his vindictive streak
is whinin' low.
He will be mellow,
too tired to think.
He will be daffy,

too desperate to know
he's all alone,
losing his charms,
losing his grip.
He will beg, borrow or steal
some measure of character
or gesture of love
tomorrow.
I see his outstretched hand,
still empty.
I am unmoved.
I am cold.
I am mean.
I've arrived at another conclusion.
He blames it on bad timing.

He is like the rest of humanity.
Humanity is like a hornet,
a flying, marching band
with jet packs and promises.
Humanity hovers like a buzzword,
a red herring we call love.
I am slow to decipher
the writing on the wall
and humanity keeps horning
its way in, burrowing, pleading
that I never think again,
that I learn to forget,
make the past a foreign place,
designate everything I know
as merely vague notions.

The Hollywood Sign

He could play
every pop song ever written
and sing too,
just well enough.
He played everyone
like the guitar.

He wanted the spotlight
but I only had one.
The burning bridges
in his wake
created a huge stumbling block
to intimacy.
He determined to climb
the Hollywood sign
one letter at a time.
He didn't jump,
but fell from grace
in a car,
like James Dean,
only not as famous.
He was up to the "D"
when Hollywood did him in.
The irony was too much for me,
up all night, crying,
trying to revive him
until I finally plowed him
beneath my contempt.

Now he is dead
though I see his name
in the paper sometimes.

God's Country

The landscape of a living room
is rough terrain
but the other guests
walk through glass doors
not feeling anything.
The sunken living room
is full of stiffs,
the hostess talking art,
wearing art, serving art,
eating art.

The other guests remind me,
one door is for coming,
one door, for going,
dare me to venture near
the gaping gap in entertainment.

A party animal may court trouble
his entire, excellent life
but where I come from
the bottom of the totem pole beckons
with a cross-hatched beaver tail
and the sea parts
to let in killer whales.

Where I come from
a tree is planted
to make you grow,

an aperture in the clouds,
like a casino's eye in the sky,
peers down at the ski lodges,
as if wondering
where the hell God went.

Neighbours

Bill

I will only speak to him in the courtyard.
He tells me everything,
how he went to the tropics
and came back with a Club Med sunburn.
Vacations as banal as your life, I think,
but Bill has always smouldered beneath
the pale, bespectacled, science-guy face.

He tends to basil and tomatoes on his balcony,
praying the siren next door will appear.
"I'll need a ladder for those legs."
Bill is dying to bury his face
in those heavenly thighs,
to take a big bite
out of that luscious ass,
dying to take her to Barbados,
get her out of that dank apartment,
far away
from the withering mother,
lace doilies, Doulton figurines,
yellowing photographs
of the war amp father,
deceased since last winter.

Charlie

Charlie thinks he's Baudelaire,
unfurls in the limelight,
hurling words on cue,
knocking back whiskies
desperate
to take me down with him.

Charlie was fluent
before word hit the street.
Charlie was trouble
before shit hit the fan.

Charlie unfurls in the limelight,
desperate to take me down with him.
I don't tell him
he's more Bukowski than Baudelaire.

Orlando

He complains, northwest coast morning light
and fashion photography do not jive.
Oh well, the pioneer spirit theme
wasn't working anyway.
We sit in his recently tiled kitchen,
sipping cappuccinos,
Orlando growing impatient
with the emaciated models,
their scatterbrained garments.
I'd be happy to be broke, he bellows,
abandoned, a sick fuck in a tacky suit
instead of a frustrated artist,
thousands of miles from home,
upwind of transcendence
no matter where I go.
The food is good,
the money is good,
but the sky is grey
above the black hole
of my conscience.
He grins. I have many stories to tell.
I look at my watch.
I want to shoot you, you know.
You have extraordinary cheekbones,
and those lips . . .

Disaster Route

I know a menace when I see one,
but some people land on me
so hard, they leave dents.

Why don't I get out of the road?
She looks like a Tin Lizzy,
always steering right,
green doors buzzing
like dragonfly wings,
flapping in my face,
you are nothing,
you are nothing.

What is wrong with me?
I court disasters
named Nicole or Christine.
They wind up as bugs
smashed all over my windshield.
I know a menace when I see one,
yet I invite them into my home,
feed them,
clothe them,
cloud their memory,
dish out coins for the bus.
Why can't I take
the scenic route instead?

The Haymakers

Waitress taps her feet,
the ground swells,
vertical blinds sway
to the Haymakers,
our blue Nash parked outside.
I feel mighty righteous
in my anaconda boots.

This is real country.
This is God's country.
This is a worldwide tour.
Who'd a thunk? Big in Paris.
We fly over Italy tomorrow,
dock on British shores next week.

The critics said
the quality of our sound
was developing at a terrific rate.
It lit up the charts one day,
bright as a newly wired house.

It's not easy,
brothers in a band,
fighting over everything,
one Nudie jacket between them.
I employ their pliers, guitars, fists.
They fix my brakes,
slip me candy,
elegant chord progressions.

Lyrics etched in wood,
our fifteen minutes nearly up.
What does it matter
how I feel about it?
I read the manuals.
They show no mercy.
Get perfect pitch or get out.

Still, I feel mighty righteous
in my anaconda boots.

Urban Forest

The approaching serenade of heat,
onslaught of noon
dissuade me
from running up the stairs.
How did I get here?
It's hot, it stinks,
no respite from concrete.
I find several arbutus
'round the reservoir,
a chain-link fence,
requisite razor wire, graffiti.
I walk there,
longing for the release of rapids,
their white noise.

In Hollywood, they say
what the camera does not see, does not exist.
My homeland is eroding
as surely as I have a conscience,
though rumour has it they are still there:
the cathedrals of Douglas fir,
harbour seals bobbing in the bay,
the whale, eagle, otter, bear.

Song of the Shirt

The rickety storefront hums
with rhythm and rage,
a chorus of aliens within.
We strain to hear their Singers,
spools hovering like bats.
Through cocoons of thread,
they croon . . .
Ladybug, ladybug,
fly away home,
Your house is on fire,
your children are alone.

At a nickel a sleeve, ten bucks
for a whole goddamn neighbourhood,
the boss can afford
to whistle while they work,
hold his belly,
chortle all the way to the bank
though he too is a slave
to his wardrobe
of loud shirts,
wages of sin.
He clean-shaves his face,
no fear of conviction
as another generation
dresses for work.

How to Live with a Bitch

When a bitch basks in the sun,
she is not worried
about Vitamin D or melanoma,
she is doing what she pleases.

When a bitch
gets blood on her bed
or powder on her nose,
she is probably quite content.

When a bitch stomps
on a hornet's nest
until she swells up,
surely, she does not feel remorse.

When a sniffy Staffordshire bitch
named Brick House
drools all over your tracks,
you'd better get out of the game.

Get used to the bitch.
You adopted her,
rescued her from the chain,
the teasing, the junkyard,
its oily, packed dirt floor.

Get used to the holes.
Holes in the walls,
holes in the couch,
holes in your motorcycle jacket
and holes in the story.
Get used to the teeth.
Get used to the smell.
Get used to being bowled over
by fifty pounds of charm
as she helps to host the parties.

Get used to slimy balls, bones, toys.
Get used to hounding,
submissive gestures,
begging and whining.
Get used to the bitch
barking out answers during *Jeopardy*.

Thank God for your bitch.
She thinks your ass smells good
and covers it much better than you can.

Sara's Svengali

She felt sorry for him,
at first,
his big honker,
snake eyes,
furry back,
stringy muscles,
Tiny Tim pathetic-*ness*.
Then, things got ugly.

He spits on her night box,
glossing over its inner workings.
He never has to feel sorry for Sara,
obscenely beautiful Sara,
acing her auditions.

He rubs his cock with coke,
reserves his tongue for puns,
rises with the moon
to come till she's undone.

Shiny, glowing with effort,
petals shuddering,
love bud craning for heat,
Sara serves herself up.

She's fit to be tied,
I'm the man for the job.
Everyone knows it.
I'm the man.

He bites her toes,
smacks her bum till it burns,
suckles at her titties,
her neck,
everyone sure to know.
Behind the 8-ball,
needful of coca,
fucked up the ass,
Needle-Always-Full-Sara
endures,
spiral of innards contracting,
expanding,
feigning eruption
at the precise moment
to meet a precise hit.

Surfing Season

Dude,
it is not quite the season to surf.
The breakers are too mellow
to heave spring forward
on a mudslide.

Paperback marriage
hangs on a hook
in the bathroom,
amulets, beads and pendants
swaying with the building.
Honeycomb tiles,
hardwood flooring
split apart to form a mouth.
All the better
to nip your feet, my dear.

The year of Saddam,
old gunfighter a diversion
from the seasons.
Fire.
Flood.
Earthquake.
Riot.
Loss a motif;
the Playboy Mansion
shedding bricks,
the dog that ran

from the gunfire,
a Shaker rocking chair,
my mother,
the light at the end
of the tunnel,
my husband,
all my charms
at the end
of warm winter
named El Duce
after the surfer.

Purple Lipstick

I am one of those women who wait . . .
wait until my husband kills me
to find new surroundings.

Reeling, I am greeted
by a bawling, two-headed calf.
A zombie named Joe
talks until my dress bleeds.
A stuffed badger
serves as a footstool,
hills look like hush puppies
and faces shine in the dark.

The men have big tits.
They are very proud
as they don purple lipstick,
splash on Brut,
billow out in black satin bras.

I was wearing yellow clogs
the day I tried to get away.
He kicked the cat off the bed,
beat up a cigarette.
The smoke in his eyes
puffed out in rings
as he blurted, "I need to eat,
or drink, or punch somebody,
even if I don't mean it."

If Wishes Had Bones

The men in blue are called inside
to guard a thread of life,
phone off the hook,
line outside quivering.

They hold the hooded mob at bay,
whisper questions
to shadows on the wall
that only billow,
dance and allude
to the disaster next door,
distant as live satellite news.

The men in blue
wish and pray and chant:
I want to burn for you,
a night of healing light.
Nothing happens.
They polish a box of baby shoes,
paint finger paintings.
Nothing happens.
They inhale beeswax,
split a wishbone with their pinkies.
Still, nothing.

On the mantel,
a red-winged blackbird
crows the end of magic.

Now is the time
to rein in our dreams.
The walls fall down.
The trees fall down.
Finally, the truth falls down
like birds, wings dissected.
If wishes had bones,
I could walk away.

Strange fruit lures many ghouls
to the last tree in the yard,
the one that lost its working limbs,
bears an effigy instead.

stanley park

a circular drive
under heaven's trees
rusty Volvo
bivouacked
golden boy
golden tongue
long limbs
tawny eyes
butterscotch mouth
low sighs
long hands
high tied
pipe dreams
harboured
within

Long Road

I've come a long way to see
pleasure boaters swilling beer,
water taxi nymphs
ferrying mountain climbers
across Howe Sound Corridor,
low grey sky
affording little headroom.

I've come a long way to see
the island that looks like a dragon,
twin platelets shivering in the mist,
an anvil for a head.
Cyclists puff by
cottages with pink bows,
dwarfed now by dishes of satellite news.

Raven raiders plunder a patch of corn,
sandpipers skittle through the waves,
cormorant perches on a piling,
flocks of mallards wheeze squeeze-toy noises
while a group of birders
gather 'round a telescope on a tripod
seeking the exotic.

I've come a long way
to find a burr in my stocking,
to see the signs of home:
Quiet—Doll Hospital
Bird Refuge Ahead
Realtor on Duty
STOP

New Lover

Shacked up, knocked up,
an experiment in coupling,
banality and hormones,
honeymoon over by noon.
Not
in my lifetime
but you lie on me
like an instrument.
The solution is to unwind
according to the knowledge of rap.
Unwind the kinks,
vent weirdness from within,
take it to the lawn if necessary.

I can take it.
You presume too much,
got your virgins and whores
all mixed up
and I'm not your mother.

I've seen fragments:
a lonely cock ring,
handcuffs idling on the dresser.
I've seen gestures:
fists around wrists,
arms overhead,
a smack on the bottom,
some lame-assed lyrics.

I want to see you
tie me
to your timber bed,
hear you confess.

backroads

hawk and wires
leaning shacks
I remember
the creaky mill
swayback mule
lone blue heron
poplar stands
catching the wind
bees quilted
birds' feet
sown
fox thievery
Father's geese
pink smoke
signals
fences'
end

Divorce from the Divine

He is the saviour
of his family,
first born male heir,
prince among men,
divined by God; his race,
sport, religion, nation,
tribe, century.
My fate
is divined by him,
golden boy.

Before we had each other,
I worked out with dumbbells,
my mattress stuffed with dreams.
It's taken about six years
to trash the place,
eat each other's livers.

The strength of men is conspicuous.
Mine manifests itself
on an altar in my bedroom,
sullen, obscene, gloating,
beside a photograph of the snowy egrets
we encountered in Palm Springs.
We were rent asunder
there and then
but here I sit,
waiting for the final blow.

My plumpness has returned,
a vestige of my soul.
I put salt on the table,
have an appetite
for something other than crow.

Beware of Dogshit

Fat ass pounding on the porch above.
Cold tea, cold lover,
big dog, big dog shit.
The logic around here
is like a lizard
flashing across hot rocks.

Never live with the landlord.
Say everything twice.
Everything.
He wants to live in a parallel universe
where fate would govern our lives
in a kinder, gentler fashion.
They are not lies to him.

The painted desert used to beckon.
So did pussy,
but with his one-trick pony dick
put out to pasture,
he has become a boar,
more roar than tusk.

A Communist horde,
the queer nation,
a roster of rock stars,
errant royal family members,
a colony of lepers
and we, his tenants,

have shown up
at the door of the castle
at one time or another,
not exactly begging,
but in need.
Heat would be nice.
He growls, slams the door,
politically correct enough
to never use the "N" word
though he treats us like niggers.

The hunt for meaning continues.
A tiny robin's nest
sits high on a bookshelf
to remind him
of his love of children.
Girlfriend Carla
drizzles bittersweet chocolate
over his strawberries,
a new ring through her nose
every Christmas.

Scarecrow

On our knees,
on the sly,
between St. Nick
in the starry sky,
the Virgin on the dash,
we pray, for oblivion.

Poolside palms,
smoking jacket,
black velvet Elvis,
our silhouettes on brocade walls,
you take joy,
elephantine joy.
You sear my armour,
bite life on the neck,
bruise the veil.

In the bath you say,
I love your curves.
My arms elongated like tentacles
reach down to envelope
your long, lean body,
our painful history
drummed from your head.

I could brave anything then:
July, millstones,
sweet peas growing on chains,
crows in the garden.

I could bear anyone then,
anyone but a coward,
anyone but a dummy,
anyone but us.

I want to possess the past,
the way a blind hawk hunts.
I want remembrance,
followed by a long siesta
on the motel bed,
danger past, dread over.
Just when you think it's gone forever,
meaning happens.

You stand in the sunshine,
straw hat instead of shades.
We suit each other at last,
sprinkle holy water
on our dream home,
goats, motorcycles in the yard,
offspring trampling the vegetables.

There is nothing greater
than yellow broom
on the hillside
or the rawness you cradle
in your arms each night.

Valentine's Day

I was supposed to meet
me dear old foster mum
at the beauty parlour that day.
Dig that beehive.
Mona's so goddamned old
she calls it the *beauty parlour.*
She's either sitting under a hair dryer,
blowin' her beer-soaked brain cells dry,
or in the beer parlour gettin' tanked.
She's so goddamned old,
she calls it the *beer parlour.*
Oh, but she goes in
the *Ladies and Escorts* entrance.
Ladies! Hah!
You ever check out the losers
in that scum-hole?
It stinks.

I didn't feel like meetin' the old bag
and her new blue rinse. Okay?
I met my friends
at the mall instead. Okay?
Is that okay with you?
Since when is hangin'
with your friends against the law?
I don't need no alibi.

School? Fuck that. I hate school.
I skipped school that day.
What the hell
am I going to learn in school?
The world's a mess
and it's all *your* fault?
Bookstore? Hey, I don't hang
in no friggin' bookstores.
Do I look like Snow White to you?
"G?" This letter?
This letter right here?
What does it mean to you?
No, you moron,
it don't stand for *Georgetown*.
It stands for *Gangsta*.
Gangsta Girl.

Cop cubicle hazy with cigarette smoke.
Asshole won't let me light up though.
Reeks of Old Spice too,
makes me want to puke.

Reluctantly, she recalls
the taxi driver's
bright orange turban,
blank, brown face
as he lay
among the reeds and snapdragons,
wind hurling snow,
a harsh flurry.

Come on,
let's go to the party.
It's been a long, hard winter,
more carnage than usual.
I want to go someplace warm.
I hate this fuckin' cow town
in the middle of nowhere.

They drive back
through a warren of snowbanks,
a stand of pines on the edge of town,
grim and silent for once,
banter thudding to the floor.

It was his own fault.
He blew it.
Fuckin' raghead thought he was a stud.
Probably thought we were little daisies
or something, ripe for the picking.
Probably thought
he was going to live out
his favourite fucking sex-u-al fantasy.
Three at once, eh?
Except, he's the one who gets stabbed,
he's the one who gets fucked!
Hey, it was a gangbang, only in reverse.
Hah!

His slippers fall off.
Still in the car.
G-girls don't know what to do
with the bloody things.

In the road,
a four-legged fur creature,
a culprit, chicken in its mouth,
lacy splotches of thin blood
all over the snow, like a valentine.
Girls try to stop,
spin round and round,
gun it, barrel sideways
into a deep drift.
Gangsta girls laugh.
What the fuck was that?
It was a fuckin' wolf!
Hey, girl! Did you hit him?
Nah, he ran off.
It's too puny to be a wolf. It's a coyote.
Wow! That was amazing.
Go for it, Wile E.
This has been one fuckin' righteous day, man.

It was so cold the blood got sticky.
He got pale too, snowflakes falling,
melting into the black pools of pupil.
Who is this guy? Does he have a wife?
Is she sitting at home right now, waiting,
cursing him out
because his dinner's getting cold?
No tears on my pillow, that's for sure.

This town.
I know this town's
supposed to be quaint and all,
at least that's what they tell the tourists.
Fucking tourists,
in their fucking white Stetsons.
Cowboys.
There ain't no fucking cowboys
in this town.
Never even seen a cowboy.
It's a joke.

This town.
An essential fury
always layin' low,
like a grizzly bear in hibernation.

Hey, I need it.
I need it to survive.
I need this rage,
this *fucking* rage,
pure as the driven snow.
Like me.

Maternal Instincts

Three months along, still disconnected
from that which we have conjured,
we three leave the Big Smoke
to visit Norma,
the formidable redhead,
the widow from Lund.
John says, She shoots at kayakers,
but only the rude ones.
We get lost, together,
but all roads lead to Desolation Sound.
The hills have scars,
buzz-cut clear cuts,
the mark of Zorro
slashed and burned
onto mountains
with miles-wide mohawks.

We arrive at the isthmus,
"a narrow piece of land
connecting two large bodies of water,"
Norma caretaking the designer home.
Wonder when my maternal instincts
will kick in.

She dotes on us,
rustling up strawberries and waffles
for breakfast
and a feast of oysters swimming in butter

for dinner.
Norma says movies are not art,
claims not to miss them.

There is no moon,
no light at all, until
Norma begins *kicking the stars*
on the beach,
so we may find our way back
via bioluminescence.

The next day I spy jays, hawks
and ruby-throated hummingbirds.
John goes overboard,
sees a mermaid in the cove.
John always sees things,
even when he's not looking.

Junior

The trophies of a rugged individual
line the den of his brain.
He is blessed with sea legs,
a pair of itchy feet,
an eye drawn
to the night sky
like a sextant.
The Great Pyramids are next.

Junior knows he was an accident,
his life a voyage
beset with flukes,
jolly uncles
reeking of onions and beer.

He is a frantic boy,
anxious to leave,
man on a mission,
ferreting out
the least known inhabitants
of the house.

Junior can bamboozle
his father out of anything,
Dad's whiskers enshrined
within a rusty tobacco tin
in the tree fort,
like some hairy morality tale.

The glowing bed gives Junior away,
under the covers with the tiny, silver Maglite
Dad bought at the Mountain Equipment store.

Junior favours high sea adventures,
cold, Northern latitudes and ex-convicts
working the salmon fishery.
The baneful captain,
a crucifixion in his face,
haunted Junior every night for a month.

He is over the hump now,
sitting atop his perch
in the dining room,
daydreaming,
the chowder cold.
"Thar she blows!"
Junior spies the great blue whale
breaching whitecaps
in a black sea of stars.

Willow Garden

Lazy river, bed of roses,
blue butterflies float above
black currant grapes,
leave tiny rings
of white powder
on the fruit,
early morning traces of grace.
The willow reminds me
of our mother.
Like all mothers,
she was beautiful once.

The kettle whistles,
her ashes upon my sister's mantel,
though Martha swears
to see her in the garden
nearly every morning.
Her spine stiffens,
recalling our mother's deeds.

I left home to forget, remember?
To search and destroy.
I left home with a burning belief
in nothing,
including punk rock.
I have come to curse the day
I entered the surf
at the deep end of California,

the way I refused
to come up for air.

It was always too soon
or never enough,
but she waited,
knowing I was so much like her,
that river or ocean,
I would not drown,
not all at once.

Day-Long Hour on Killarney Lake Trail

About all we could stand,
we, allsorts of *extended family*,
together by fluke,
forsaken access rights,
errant mothers,
befuddled fathers,
mobile phone calls through days
of yuletide windstorms and blackouts.

Thirteen-mile island,
twenty minutes on the ferry.
Does it have video games?
My son needs to know, in case
the panting, pawing salty dog ocean
or mugging-for-the-camera mountains
fail to amuse him.
He brought me a nosegay of dandelions
this morning, sat down to Honey-Nut Cheerios,
the Sports section and *Cars For Sale* ads.
At least he's reading.
Eight-year-old wisenheimer
in a *Rat Fink Cruisin' Canada* tee shirt,
arguing with his buddy
over which skinny little arse
will sit where
in the back seat of the Jeep.

He wants to decide,
but Randy carries just as much ammunition
—a Game Boy Colour in glaring green—though
Junior has a Game Boy Advance *and* a PlayStation 2.
His Game Boy Colour—screaming yellow—
was nicked from our car after the accident.
Thievery unnerves him. Some things are hard
to explain to a child, like Winona Ryder,
researching a role. Hope she never plays a terrorist.

Junior assails Randy and Caitlin,
along-for-the-ride
teenaged niece by failed marriage,
with a report on BMW Roadster stats,
the debut of the Mercury Marauder.
A Porsche Boxter, maybe,
but not a Dodge Ram,
they burn way too much gas.
I have three hundred
and fifty-three dollars
and sixty-five cents saved up.
Caitlin smiles, cranks up the volume
of a portable CD player,
tuning out the pimp-killing dad
afraid to touch his daughter.

Junior balks at four kilometres around Killarney Lake,
no matter how invigorating the hike, or beautiful the day—
forest cloaked in cloud, mist icing a still water cake top.
Josef, long suffering über step-dad tells him we are going
to navigate a circle—more or less—around the lake,

just like a racetrack. Junior zooms ahead,
bossing Randy and Brinda—*Brinda Bonkers*,
purebred brindle and white, piss-and-vinegar,
too-big-for-her-collar Staffy,
deftly dodging Junior and his feet.
He tosses off his jacket.
I'm hot. Carry it for me.
No, it's your responsibility.
No, it's not.
Yes, it is.
No, it's not.
Yes, it is. I will not treat you like a baby.
Junior drags it through mud,
pine needle mash,
throws it to the ground.
Pick it up.
No!
Fine, you will pay for that jacket
if I have to replace it.
Fifty bucks.
He picks it up.
Bitches, whines, moans, whimpers.
My back hurts,
pitching into his old man parody.
Ow, ow, ow, oooowww.
Where, how does your back hurt?
I don't know, it just does.
What do you want us to do?
Sit. I have to sit. I can't walk.
Okay, let's sit.
He finds a moist, furry log and parks it.

Ow, ow, ow, oooowww.
The hour marches on.

Caitlin swears Junior is an actor,
deigns to give him a piggyback ride.
Spitting Spiderman dialogue at her ear,
the pain miraculously disappears,
me toting his boots,
Josef his jacket.

HEATHER HALEY was born in Matapedia, Quebec, and raised in Manitoba, the Kootenays and Cloverdale, B.C. She was employed for many years as a staff writer, editor and arts reviewer for the *LA Weekly* before returning to Canada in 1993. Heather also published *Rattler*, a critically acclaimed multimedia arts and literary journal and her work has appeared in numerous North American publications: the *Antigonish Review*, *Coe Review*, *Northern Lights*, *Literary Storefront*, *subTerrain*, *On The Bus*, *Heresies*, *High Performance*, *Medusa*, *Verb*, *Arts Vancouver* and the Manic D Press anthology, *The Verdict Is In*. Find her online at: *Bard's Ink*, *Treeline*, the Edgewise Café and e-poets.net. Architect of the Edgewise ElectroLit Centre and the Vancouver Videopoem Festival, she has appeared at the Vancouver Press Club, Kootenay School of Writing, Word on the Street Festival and on Bravo TV's *Book Television*. In a previous incarnation she fronted and wrote songs for The .45s, with Randy Rampage, and the all-girl band, The Zellots. Heather's first videopoem, *Dying for the Pleasure*, is currently touring the film festival circuit.